HANDEL
AND HIS
AUTOGRAPHS

A. HYATT KING

Published by the
Trustees of the British Museum
London 1967

PRINTED IN GREAT BRITAIN
AT THE UNIVERSITY PRESS, OXFORD
BY VIVIAN RIDLER
PRINTER TO THE UNIVERSITY

LIST OF ILLUSTRATIONS

Plate I is reproduced by courtesy of Mr. Gerald Coke, plate VI*a* and plate XIV by courtesy of the Syndics of the Fitzwilliam Museum, Cambridge. All the other plates and the frontispiece are reproduced from originals in the Royal Music Library in the British Museum

3

The music, with Handel's signature, reproduced on the cover is part of folio 58 verso of the autograph of the Concerto Grosso in E minor Op. 6, No. 3, 1739 (R.M. 20. g. 11)

HANDEL AND HIS AUTOGRAPHS

On 27 November 1957 Queen Elizabeth II presented to the Trustees of the British Museum the Royal Music Library, which had been deposited on loan in the Museum since 1911. The occasion of this munificence was the two hundredth anniversary of another royal gift to the Trustees, that of the Old Royal Library which King George II had presented in 1757.

By far the most important and interesting part of the Royal Music Library consists of the collection of Handel autograph scores. Although they have long been studied and used by scholars, their existence is hardly known to thousands of music-lovers who enjoy Handel's music. The purpose of this booklet is to give some account of the history and use of these autographs from the composer's time until their presentation to the British Museum, and to show how they reveal something of his life and character and shed light on his habit and method of working.

The first mention of the autographs is found in Handel's will, which he wrote out and signed with his own hand on 1 June 1750. The relevant clause is as follows:

I give and bequeath to Mr. Christopher Smith my large harpsicord, my little House Organ, my Musick Books, and five hundred Pounds sterl:

The 'Musick Books' probably included, besides the autograph scores, a considerable quantity of early manuscript copies now in the Royal Music Library, in the State and University Library at Hamburg, and elsewhere. For most of the purposes of this booklet, however, it will be convenient to equate these 'books' with the autographs, including that portion of them which, as will be explained later, soon became separated from the main collection and is now in the Fitzwilliam Museum at Cambridge.

The early transmission of the 'Musick Books' long posed a problem because of an apparent ambiguity in Handel's will, and because there were two men, father and son, both known as 'Christopher Smith'. The father, born at Ansbach as Johann Christoph

Schmidt, was Handel's compatriot, whom he brought from Germany to England, at some time between 1716 and 1719, to act as his secretary. Schmidt, who seems to have anglicized his name as early as 1720, later became Handel's close personal friend, business associate, and principal copyist. He died in London in 1763. His son, John Christopher (b. 1712, d. 1795), joined his father in 1720 and became Handel's pupil when only thirteen years old. Later he was also taught by Pepusch and Roseingrave: he soon made his mark as a composer of opera and oratorio. When Handel's sight began to fail from about 1750 onwards, the younger Smith helped him with his oratorio performances. Either the father or the son would thus have been a worthy beneficiary under Handel's will, of which there are two copies, the official (Probate) copy and the private copy, both written in his own hand.

The original uncertainty is due to the fact that in neither copy did Handel finally specify which 'Christopher Smith' he intended to inherit the 'Musick Books'. Moreover, in the private copy he wrote the word 'Senior', possibly as an addition, after the name 'Smith' (pl. 1) and later deleted it. (This word does not occur in the Probate copy.) The identity of the legatee was not conclusively proved until 1955 when Dr. James Hall succeeded in tracing the elder Smith's will, proved on 10 January 1763, from which the following clause may be quoted: 'I give & bequeath unto my son John Christopher Smith All my Music Books and Peices of Musick whether Manuscript or otherwise which were left to me by the last Will & Testament of my Friend George Frederick Handel deceased.'

We may never know for certain what caused Handel to vacillate, but there may have been some truth in a story in the anonymous *Anecdotes of George Frederick Handel and John Christopher Smith* (1799), a work which is the primary source for much of the early history of the 'Musick Books'. It states that, about four years before Handel's death on 14 April 1759, there was a quarrel and total estrangement between him and the elder Smith, and that the composer consequently threatened to substitute the son's name in his will; a reconciliation was, however, effected by the son some three weeks before Handel died.

He seems at one time to have entertained a different plan for disposing of his 'Musick Books', because there is another story (again found only in the *Anecdotes*), according to which

it had been Handel's wish that all the manuscript music should be assigned to Oxford, and preserved in the university library; and with that attention to his posthumous fame, and regard to an university which had been sensible of his merits, he proposed to give Smith a legacy of three thousand pounds, if he would resign his claim to the promise which Handel had made to him. But he had too much enthusiasm for the art, and too great veneration for the production of so able a composer, his friend and instructor, to relinquish for any pecuniary consideration so estimable a prize; and Handel faithfully fulfilled his promise at his death.

The *Anecdotes* also tell us of an interesting destination to which the 'Musick Books' might have gone later. For Smith received, presumably between 1759 and 1763, a tempting proposal of an unusual kind: 'The Great Frederick, King of Prussia, offered Smith two thousand pounds for Handel's manuscripts: but he was unwilling to let such a treasure go out of England.'

In the event, neither of the Smiths enjoyed possession of the autographs for very long. The elder owned them for little less than four years, from Handel's death until his own, and the younger for little more than eleven. Moreover, it seems likely that during the ownership of one or the other, a certain portion of the 'Musick Books' became separated, as mentioned above, and now forms part of the Founder's Collection in the Fitzwilliam Museum. This portion, in terms of volumes, amounted to a little more than one-twelfth of the whole, the royal collection originally comprising eighty-eight volumes and the Fitzwilliam group seven.

Although the latter includes about a dozen complete compositions in the smaller forms, the reason for the separation is fairly clear. The portion detached seemed at that time to be of relatively slight importance. For it consisted mostly of sketches, fragments of unfinished works and sections of finished works which had become separated from them and could not be identified for reassembly. There are some volumes in the royal collection containing similar material (cf. pl. II and pl. III).

7

During Handel's last years, when he was nearly blind and probably estranged from the elder Smith, his 'Musick Books' may well have fallen into some confusion. Whole quires may have become detached from complete but unbound works, and sketches and fragments from any pieces to which they were related. Such confusion could have facilitated the ultimate division of the music, which probably took place fairly soon after Handel's death, while his estate was being cleared up and during the ownership of the elder Smith. But it also seems possible that the collection remained intact until after his decease, and was divided only when his son offered it to King George III. Although we shall probably never know who became the temporary owner of the smaller portion and offered it to Lord Fitzwilliam, the latter was an eminently suitable recipient as an ardent Handelian, and one of the chief sponsors of the Handel Festival of 1784. Since he had the tidy habit of dating books added to his library, we know that in 1778 he acquired one volume of Handel autographs, containing the 'Chandos' anthem 'O praise the Lord', and in 1799 the other six volumes, comprising sketches, rough drafts, and fragments.

The younger Smith's ownership came to an end in unusual circumstances, the story of which again is found only in the *Anecdotes*. It runs as follows:

The Princess Dowager of Wales having expressed an inclination to engage some person of eminence in the musical profession, to attend twice a week and give her instruction on the harpsichord, Lord Bute said that he would recommend a master who he was sure would be acceptable; but before he could name him, Her Royal Highness interrupting him, said, she had already fixed on a person; and immediately mentioned Mr. Smith. He was accordingly placed in the Princess's household, and attended at Carlton House once or twice a week, with a salary of two hundred pounds. . . . After the death of the Princess Dowager [in 1774], the King graciously continued to Mr. Smith the same pension out of his privy purse, free of all deductions, which greatly contributed to the ease and comfort of his life. In a mind so constituted as that of Mr. Smith, where liberality and disinterestedness were distinguishing features, it is easy to be supposed that gratitude would be no less conspicuous. . . . He accordingly expressed that gratitude in a way he thought most acceptable

8

to his Sovereign; and in the fulness of his heartfelt acknowledgment, presented to the King the rich legacy which Handel had left him, of all his manuscript music, in score.

This narrative has long been accepted without question. While there is no reason to doubt its substantial accuracy, there are one or two points which call for comment. Smith's name does not appear in the printed lists of the Household of Augusta, Princess Dowager of Wales (as given in the Royal Kalendars), nor in the sovereign's papers. Smith may, of course, have been technically in the Princess's private employment, but for such a status, requiring an attendance of only twice a week, a salary of £200 a year seems rather high. It is the same as Handel himself had received some forty years earlier when appointed music-master to three of the royal Princesses, Anne, Amelia, and Caroline, in 1728. There is, moreover, no record in King George III's papers of the payment of Smith's pension, which he would have received for nearly twenty years, until his death in 1795. (Unfortunately, the lists of pensioners for this period are incomplete.)

Despite this chequered history and so many points of uncertainty, the 'Musick Books' did pass into royal ownership, presumably not long after the Princess's death in 1774. The possession of this treasure must have given great satisfaction to the King and to his consort Queen Charlotte, for they were both amateurs of music and had long been admirers of Handel. But it seems likely that before long their Majesties must have realized that ownership of this unique property carried a certain responsibility. For in the late 1770s (especially after the sale of William Boyce's great library in 1778), musical manuscripts were beginning to arouse interest at auction sales. A large collection of autograph scores in the hand of a great master was clearly something irreplaceable and of great price. Moreover, these manuscripts were still unbound, many of them in loose quires and sheets, which could easily have been lost or damaged by careless handling. Wherever they may have been stored, there were the ever-present risks of fire and damp inseparable from an old building in the eighteenth century.

When the King accepted the collection from Smith, he could

hardly have foreseen how imminent was its use by a musical scholar, Charles Burney, the forerunner of many others. George III and the Queen, who actively shared his interest in all the royal music, could not have postponed indefinitely some action to solve the twin problems familiar to all owners of valuable books—conservation and security. Regarding the housing of the royal music in general, we know nothing certain until well into the nineteenth century. In the later eighteenth, it is possible that it was scattered in various royal residences—Windsor Castle, St. James's Palace, and Buckingham House. We are better informed about their binding, within certain rather wide chronological limits.

We know that the man partly responsible was Frederick Nicolay, who had been appointed Queen Charlotte's Page of the Back Stairs (a highly responsible appointment in her household), in 1762, and, from about 1780 onwards, her Principal Page. He was also in fact, though not by title, her music librarian. The proof of Nicolay's connexion with the Handel manuscripts is found in his annotations. Although they are not signed, the handwriting can be shown, by comparison with Nicolay's autograph will, to be his. These annotations, written on over fifty sheets, have been bound in with the quires of the autographs and a few early manuscript copies, and must therefore have been written before the binding was done. Nicolay's purpose in writing most of the annotations was to draw attention to gaps in the autographs (pl. IV) which he must have collated with early copies or printed scores.

This strongly suggests, but does not prove, that Nicolay exercised some measure of control over the binding of the Handel autographs and probably of some of the copies. The style is simple, but dignified —half-red morocco leather, gilt lettering, and tooling on the spine, the titles of the works mostly lettered on black pieces, and sides of marbled paper. It is sometimes possible to date bindings with fair precision from the tools used, but unfortunately those employed for binding this music were in use from the early 1780s until about 1805. The earlier part of this period seems the more likely, for two reasons: first, the obviously urgent need for conservation; secondly, the use of an almost identical style for binding over one hundred books of printed music, of which those belonging to Queen Charlotte bear on the end-papers, in Nicolay's hand, her name and the date 1788. But the considerable task of binding the Handel autographs in eighty-eight volumes would probably have been spread over several years.

How far Nicolay was responsible for the way in which the Royal binder treated these autographs, is debatable. At all events, the results left a good deal to be desired. Instructions must have been given to the binder to bind as many volumes as possible to a uniform size, which was made all the easier by Handel's preference for using oblong folio music-paper with ten staves to a page. After trimming, the pages measured, on the average, between 11 and 12 inches long and 9 and 10 inches tall. In many volumes the binder trimmed the sheets so heavily that some of the music or words which Handel often wrote in the margins have been lost, as can be seen on the upper part of plate x and the lower part of plate xiii. In some cases, however, where this overflow of inspiration ran to the extreme of the fore-edge, the binder noticed and trimmed round it, thus leaving an awkward tab perhaps an inch or so deep, jutting out a quarter of an inch or more (pl. v).

The royal acquisition of the Handel autographs coincided roughly with the time when musical history was first written in England. For it was in the early 1770s that Dr. Charles Burney and Sir John Hawkins began to collect material for their great rival books. The former's *History* was published in four volumes, from 1776 to 1789, the latter's in five volumes, all printed in 1776. Naturally Handel, the over-whelming figure in the age just past, was treated at length by both authors, but much more so by Burney than Hawkins. There is no evidence that the latter consulted the Handel autographs; but there is plenty that Burney did. It is quite clear from his correspondence with his daughter Fanny, who had been appointed one of the 'Keepers of the Robes' to Queen Charlotte in 1786, that he asked her to use her influence to obtain permission from the King to borrow the autographs of the operas, and perhaps of other works as well.

In his *History*, Burney uses such phrases as 'having been indulged an opportunity of examining it in the autograph score at leisure'. Indeed, he went so far as to write his comments on several leaves, in *Scipione* and *Siroe* (in pencil), and in ink on a slip bound in later into the autograph of *Ezio*.

General interest in Handel was further stimulated by the great Festival of 1784, two years after which, on 25 May 1786, Dr. Samuel Arnold issued his first prospectus for a complete edition of Handel's works. Such an edition depended for its accuracy on his having obtained access to the autographs, but this Arnold apparently failed to do. His failure is all the more extraordinary because he was able to secure permission to dedicate the edition to King George III and seems to have been encouraged by him. The merits and defects of the edition can hardly be discussed here, but the latter are partly due to Arnold's lack of access to the autographs. His proposal for a revised edition was cut short by his death: it is not clear whether he intended to remedy his previous failure.

The next generation of scholars, the editors appointed by the English Handel Society, was more fortunate. From their very first publication—the 'Coronation' Anthems, edited by Crotch in 1843—they were granted permission by Queen Victoria to use the originals. Although their venture ran into difficulties and ceased in 1858 after only sixteen volumes had been issued, all were edited from the autographs.

As already stated, there is no clear evidence as to where the Handel autographs were kept in Burney's time. His letters (already mentioned) to his daughter Fanny were addressed to her with the Court at Windsor Castle. A little later, it seems probable that the autographs were kept at Buckingham Palace. They were certainly there by the time of Queen Victoria's accession, and it is from the early 1850s that we have what seems to be the first known description of them, from the pen of Victor Schoelcher, a French specialist in Handel, whose somewhat highly coloured biography appeared in an English translation in 1857. The passage is as follows:

It [the collection] is in the royal palace of London, but not lodged there, it must be confessed, in a royal style. Buried in a sort of private office, and still kept in its poor original binding, it is concealed from all the world, and, I may say (using the figurative expression of the old nursery tale) that if I were the Queen, I should have those precious volumes bound in crimson velvet, mounted with gold, and I should have a beautiful cabinet to hold them, which should be surmounted by Roubiliac's fine bust, and supported by four statues of white marble, representing Sacred and Profane Music, Moral Courage and Honesty. This I should place in the Throne Room of my palace, proclaiming by this means that it is one of the most invaluable jewels of the English Crown.

The 'private office' referred to was probably the room of George Frederick Anderson, who was Master of the Queen's Music from 1848 to 1870, and to whom Schoelcher makes acknowledgement in his preface. In it he also thanks not, as might be expected, Queen Victoria, but Prince Albert for granting permission to copy from the autographs, which he studied for over a month. Besides writing his biography of Handel, Schoelcher had another, much bigger aim, which was to compile 'the most complete catalogue of his works which has yet appeared'. (This catalogue, though nearly completed, has never been published: it remains in manuscript in the Music Department of the Bibliothèque Nationale in Paris.)

In the preface to his biography, Schoelcher acknowledges that all the research for the catalogue which had to be done at Buckingham Palace was entrusted to Rophino Lacy, an Irish actor, violinist, and popular dramatist, who apparently had an intimate knowledge of Handel's music which Schoelcher himself, as 'no professed musician', lacked. Here it may be mentioned that in 1856 Schoelcher acquired a collection of 129 contemporary manuscript scores of Handel which, since they contain additions in Handel's hand, may have formed part of the 'Musick Books' bequeathed to the elder Smith. According to Sir George Macfarren, in his preface to Novello's vocal score of *Belshazzar* (1873), Schoelcher later offered the scores for sale to the Trustees of the British Museum. After their refusal, he sold the collection in 1868, at Chrysander's instigation, to a group of Hamburg businessmen who later presented it to the Town Library (afterwards the State and University Library).

In 1868, the Directors of the Sacred Harmonic Society in London published, by permission of Queen Victoria, a lithographic facsimile of the autograph score of *Messiah*, then as now the most popular of all Handel's works. Another, less accurate, facsimile of this autograph was issued in two parts (1889, 1892) by Friederich Chrysander (the German scholar and biographer of Handel) who had previously issued a facsimile of the autograph of *Jephtha* in 1885, without any acknowledgement or mention or the source! Chrysander was also the moving spirit of the German Handel Society which had been founded in 1856 in order to publish the composer's complete works. After 1864 he became the Society's sole editor and virtually its owner. Although the autographs in Buckingham Palace were not the only source which Chrysander used, he consulted them more than anyone else during the latter part of the nineteenth century.

In this connexion, it may be added that there was published, long after Chrysander's death in 1901, an extraordinary story in which he was said to have added a considerable quantity of Handel manuscripts to the royal collection and to have been allowed to take some of the autographs back to his hotel in London, and later, even back to his home at Bergedorf. The story states that in the hotel Chrysander worked up to sixteen or even eighteen hours a day by drinking black coffee and keeping his feet in ice-cold water for part of the time. Although there is no reason to doubt Chrysander's capacity for work, it is most unlikely that he was allowed to remove any of the autographs from Buckingham Palace, and he certainly did not add any Handel manuscripts to the collection. He did, however, rather reprehensibly follow Burney's example and write some comments of his own in ink on numerous pages of a volume not, happily, of the autographs, but one of the early manuscript copies in the royal collection.

During the 1870s, the time when Chrysander was most active, an English scholar, W. S. Rockstro, was also studying Handel, and in the preface to his biography (1883) thanked the then Master of the Queen's Music, Mr. (later Sir) William G. Cusins, 'for the courtesy with which he afforded him every possible facility for subjecting the . . . autographs in the Royal Library to a minute and exhaustive examination, of indescribable value for critical purposes'. A little more will be said later about one result of this examination. Cusins himself, soon after his royal appointment in 1870, had made a comparative study of *Messiah* and published the results of his work in an able pamphlet *Handel's 'Messiah'. An examination of the original and of some contemporary MSS* (1874).

In 1893 the *Musical Times* published a series of articles on some notable English libraries of music, and in its issue for December there appeared an authoritative account of the Royal Collection written by Sir Walter Parratt, who in that year had succeeded Cusins as Master of the Queen's Music. Parratt wrote thus: 'The Royal Music Library in Buckingham Palace is to be found in a far corner of that labyrinthine building, and is approached from the main entrance through long corridors lined with royal portraits, and numerous back stairs and passages. The room itself is about 15 ft. square, somewhat high in proportion, and with books in rich red bindings on all sides.' This appears to be the first detailed description of the location of the room, and the extent of the room itself, into which at some time in the mid nineteenth century, perhaps under the Prince Consort's influence, royal music from various owners and residences had been brought together. The description of this room tallies roughly with Schoelcher's words 'a sort of private office . . . concealed from all the world', and seems pretty certainly to have served also as the office of the Master of the Queen's Music.

There are further details in the *Musical Times* for 1 July 1902. In an anonymous article entitled 'The Royal Music Library at Buckingham Palace' we read:

> Until quite recently the books were kept in glazed bookcases in a room at the back of the State Ball Room. This location—an upper story approached by a single narrow staircase—was a most unsatisfactory one. . . . Last year the cases and their contents were removed from the elevated position they had so long occupied and deposited in a fire-proof room situated in the basement.

Clearly, the authorities had at last realized the immense value of the music, but the remedy taken could hardly have rendered the collection easier of access to scholars. It is at this point that William Barclay Squire began to shape the destiny of the royal music as a whole, including the Handel autographs.

Squire had been appointed in 1885 to take charge of the collections of printed music in the British Museum, and proved himself a man of great influence, vision, and energy. When he wrote the article on 'Music Libraries' in the second edition of Grove's *Dictionary of Music* (1906), he noted the removal of the royal music as just mentioned, but later described the room as 'fire-proof but not damp-proof'. It was probably the latter condition, as much as difficult access, that induced him to make great efforts to persuade the authorities at the Palace to deposit the whole collection on permanent loan in the British Museum. King George V approved the loan in March 1911 and the transfer took place in the same year. Squire retired from the service of the Trustees in 1920, and was then appointed the first Honorary Curator of the collection. It was housed temporarily in the White Wing of the Museum, until the King Edward Building, where space had been allocated to the new Music Room, could be completed. This was, however, delayed by the First World War, and it was not until early in 1919 that the royal music was moved to the room where it is still housed.

As all previous attempts to produce a catalogue had proved fruitless, the Trustees were enjoined by King George V to prepare one. Immediately after his retirement, Squire set to work on the first volume, which was devoted entirely to the Handel manuscripts. Those which were autograph had been bound, ever since George III's time, in eighty-eight volumes. But the autographs were then brought together in such a haphazard way that considerable portions of large works such as *Rinaldo* and *Ottone* were scattered in volumes consisting of miscellaneous pieces and fragments, akin to those in the Fitzwilliam Museum. Such volumes were broken up, the portions brought together, and rebound so that the whole collection of autographs finally amounted to ninety-seven volumes. Squire, who had specialized in masters of the sixteenth and seventeenth centuries, disclaimed in his preface an 'intimate knowledge' of Handel's music. Nevertheless, with some help from expert friends, especially Percy Robinson, he produced, after six years' work, a catalogue which is still one of the foundations of Handelian scholarship. It was published just after his death in 1927. After the Royal Music Library was deposited in the British Museum, its use by musicologists increased rapidly, not least in respect of the Handel autographs which have been the basis of many scholarly editions and performances.

The circumstances in which the royal collection became in 1957 the property of the nation have already been mentioned at the beginning of this booklet. Thus, almost two centuries after Handel's death, his 'Musick Books', having passed through so many vicissitudes, were secured for posterity in a way which would surely have given great pleasure to the far-sighted composer.

This collection of Handel autographs is notable in several respects. It is by far the largest one of the autographs of any of the great musicians of the past now preserved in a single institution anywhere in the world. It amounts to some ninety per cent. of the total extant. (The remainder are: the seven volumes preserved in the Fitzwilliam Museum, now rebound in fifteen; half-a-dozen works in the Department of Manuscripts in the British Museum; about as many again—mostly small pieces—elsewhere, in various English, American, and German libraries and in a few private collections.) The distribution, by categories, of the ninety-seven volumes in the Royal Music Library can be seen from the following summary:

Anthems	6
Cantatas	8
Masques	3
Odes	2
Operas	37
Oratorios	23
Songs	1
Psalms	2
Te Deums	2
Miscellaneous Instrumental Works	5
Miscellaneous Selections, mainly vocal	8
Total	97

This represents about four-fifths of all the music that Handel wrote. The scope of the collection is most interesting. The autographs cover nearly fifty years of Handel's creative life, from *c.* 1702 to 1751. When he came to England on his first visit in 1710, he had eight years of fairly continuous composing behind him—the time of his sojourn in Hamburg and of his journey to Italy. It is not, perhaps, surprising that some autographs, notably those of the four Hamburg operas and one Passion (the 'St. John' is not by Handel) are lost. But it seems that Handel made some attempt to preserve his autographs as a young man, because the royal collection includes a dozen or so works written before 1710: others are in the Fitzwilliam collection. After that date, relatively little is missing. This argues a strengthened habit of conservation remarkable in a man whose life was, with few breaks, a continuous round of composing, conducting, and rehearsing, and subject especially to the pressures which are inseparable from work for the stage.

As Handel's output grew, the quantity of scores in his possession increased also. It is pertinent to ask several questions—why did he keep them so carefully? How did he store them? Who gave him the help he needed to look after them? To some extent, the answers to all these questions are interdependent, although the answer to each of the last two is conjectural. The main reason for the preservation of the autographs seems fairly clear. Handel, as a busy practical musician, needed them partly as a record of the original performance (including successive changes in the music, and, often, the names of the singers) and partly as a source from which performing material could be produced by hand, sometimes in haste. In this process the elder Smith undoubtedly played a big part, as one of the principal copyists. There is an interesting note—not, however, in Handel's writing—on folio 120 of the third volume of Anthems (R.M. 20. d. 8), reading: 'For Mr. Smith to be left at Mr. Linikey's att ye White Hart in ye Hay Market with speed.' It seems, moreover, a reasonable conjecture that Smith, being also Handel's close friend and business associate, may have helped him to keep the autographs in order. (Orderly storage of the sheets was all the more necessary if we remember that the autographs as now bound run to about nine linear feet of shelf space.) Handel was also glad to have his scores at hand as a source for self-borrowing.

It is certain that the autographs were still unbound when they passed into royal possession, fifteen years or so after Handel's death. But in some of the volumes which are now not too tightly bound stab-holes near the spine can be discerned. It is therefore possible that the quires were frequently secured with thread passed through these holes. Even so, without a proper binding, it would not have been easy to store the quires of music vertically. It may not be without significance that in many works the recto (or outer side) of the first leaf is ingrained with dirt. This suggests that the unbound sheets were shelved not vertically, but horizontally, in piles. If a work happened to be on top of a little-used pile, the surface of its first page would soon become very dirty.

One might hope to find some support for this conjecture in the inventory of Handel's household effects made after his death. But the only items of furniture possibly relevant are 'In the Clossett a large nest of Drawers' and 'In the Back Parlor a Small Deal Bookcase'. As the inventory seems, however, not to be complete, the lack of any precisely described piece of furniture suitable for storage is inconclusive. Whatever the method of storage, and whether the quires were stabbed and threaded or not, it was sometimes all too easy for the autograph of a work to become scattered. The four sections comprising that of *Alceste*, for example, are to be found in four volumes in the British Museum—three in the royal music, and one in the Department of Manuscripts.

It is strange that Handel seldom foliated manuscripts of his larger works, as an aid to keeping them in order. Only three autographs, those of *Messiah*, the *Occasional Oratorio*, and the Utrecht 'Te Deum' and 'Jubilate' bear foliation throughout which is certainly in his hand. *Belshazzar* bears partial foliation. That of *Samson* and *Joshua* is probably not Handel's. Sometimes he wrote a partial foliation, as in the autograph of *Hercules*, in which he numbered every quire, that is every eighth side. (Sometimes the numbered quire had only four sides.) One Handelian authority, Mr. Winton

Dean, believes that in the late 1740s, at the time of the completion of *Solomon* (1748), the composer 'kept a store of loose instrumental pieces which he shuffled in and out of his larger works, as the spirit moved him'. This accords with the idea that Handel, while keeping the bulk of his autographs in good order, seems to have had a mass of fragments and sketches in no order at all.

Indeed it is fairly certain that the sheets bearing the latter were often lying about in Handel's work-room and were picked up at random. The evidence for this is to be found on several leaves, all now in the Fitzwilliam Museum. They are of great interest for the human as well as the musical side of the composer who sometimes used the blank space on them for casual memoranda. On a leaf containing the autograph of a recitative in *Samson*, there occurs, written upside-down, what appears to be a memorandum of a copyist's bill for the singers' parts (assuming the figures to represent the number of pages):

Samson	140
Micah	97
Manoah	76
Delilah	31
Harapha	34
Messenger	10
In all	388

Another volume, consisting mainly of instrumental pieces, exercises in figured bass, and the like, has two curious memoranda. The first reads thus:

12 Gallons Port.
12 Bottles French Duke Street
Meels.

The last word may be the name of a wine merchant. The second (written, again, upside-down) reads:

James. . . . .
Banker in Lombard Street
pour M. Wesselow en France.

In a volume of miscellaneous sketches we find another kind of note:

Mr. Duval medecin in
Poland Street.

(According to Mortimer's *Universal Director*, this doctor was Francis Philip Duval, who is known to have studied medicine at Leyden University.) As this occurs at the foot of a leaf bearing an incomplete copy of an aria from the opera *Faramondo*, which was composed at the end of 1737 when Handel had not fully recovered from his first stroke, the note may well give the name of a doctor for possible consultation.

Perhaps the most famous of all these jottings is found on a much-used leaf now bound in another volume of miscellaneous sketches. The heavy creasing suggests that the leaf was at one time carried, folded, in Handel's pocket. On one side are the cryptic words 'yor wright at Lord Walpool's' (?Walpole), and there are some other words and names to which little significance can now be attached. The other half of the opposite fold has the following note: 'John Shaw, near a brandy shop St. Giles's in Tyburn Road, sells matches about', followed by the music of a London cry (pl. VI *a*). This is especially interesting in the light of what Lady Luxborough wrote to the poet Shenstone: 'The great Handel has told me that the hints of his very best songs have several of them been owing to the sounds in his ears of cries in the streets.' The same volume contains a leaf, headed, 'The Book of Kings, Ahab, Jezabel, Naboth, the Profet Elija', followed by ten staves of musical fragments. This suggests that at one time Handel was contemplating an oratorio on the subject of Elijah, which he would surely have found most congenial. There were doubtless other memoranda on sketch leaves now lost: those which have survived show clearly that Handel lived with his manuscripts around him.

The autographs of all the great composers shed a flood of light on their character, their habit and method of work, their changes of ideas, directions for performance, and the like. Those of Handel, forming so nearly complete a sequence, and covering the period from his seventeenth to his sixty-sixth year, are exceptionally illuminating. In respect of his musical handwriting, the most detailed study has been made by Rockstro who perceptively distinguished no fewer than nine different styles throughout those forty-nine years. The earliest is exemplified by the 'Laudate pueri dominum' in F, of *c.* 1702. The hand is small, and well formed in all details (pl. VII). This was followed by a large hand, characterized by big, black-headed crochets. From this derives a neater hand, more regular and with small crochets and carefully grouped semiquavers. Handel seems to have developed this when composing in Italy during the years 1707 to 1709: it is seen, for example, in the *Resurrezione* of 1708 (pl. VIII).

After Handel settled in England, his handwriting became more cursive and economical of space, as can be seen in the autographs of the Utrecht 'Te Deum', the 'Chandos' anthems, and *Radamisto*. The autographs of the group of operas composed for the Royal Academy of Music, including *Rodelinda* (pl. V), and ending with *Tolomeo* (1728), show an increasing command of speed, a quality even more marked in those of the early oratorios such as *Deborah* (pl. XI). The paralytic attack which Handel suffered in 1737 sometimes affected his writing by making it unsteady, and may have caused an aberration in the autograph of *Berenice*, where at the end of Act II he wrote the year 1736 instead of 1737.

The effects of this stroke lasted intermittently for a year or so, but in the autographs of the mid 1740s there is a complete recovery and the hand is firm (cf. pl. XVII). Early in the next decade, Handel's sight was affected by what seems to have been glaucoma, and the effect is very marked in the autograph of his last major work, *Jephtha* (1751). On folio 91 verso he wrote: 'biss hierher komen den 13 ☿ Febr. verhindert worden wegen relaxation des gesichts meines linken auges' [i.e. 'reached this point on [Wednesday] 13 Feb. Prevented from proceeding on account of the weakening of the sight of my left eye'] (pl. IX). Ten days later he wrote on folio 92 recto: 'den 23 ♄ dieses etwas besser worden wird angegangen'

22

[i.e. '[Saturday] the 23rd of this [month] a little better, started work again']. Another autograph which touches on the question of Handel's blindness is, rather strangely, that of *Agrippina* which dates from 1709. Folios 8 and 9 contain the music of the melody 'volo pronto' which Handel used again in 1757 in *The Triumph of Time and Truth*, but of which no autograph survives. He then added, in faint pencil, as can be seen in pl. x, the English words 'Pleasure's gentle zephyrs playing'. This addition (unless it was possibly prepared for an earlier, unrecorded performance of the song) lends colour to the theory that in his declining years Handel was not permanently or wholly blind, but had occasional periods of partial vision.

Here may be mentioned one unique 'autograph', that of *Deborah*, which, although only partly written by Handel himself, is the primary source for the oratorio. It was one of the least successful: it seems to have been written in rather a hurry, and with uneven inspiration. For no fewer than 26 of the 49 numbers are borrowed from Handel's own earlier works, and of these 10, and several recitatives, were written not by the composer but by one of two copyists working in turn with him. So close was this cooperation that he and the copyist must at times have sat side by side. The most important of the two[1] was Handel's amanuensis, J. C. Smith the elder, whose hand can be seen, for example, on the lower part of folio 16 recto of the autograph of *Deborah*, as shown on plate xi. Here the words on the upper six staves are written by Handel, and the notes by Smith; on the two lowest staves, the procedure is reversed. This extraordinary alternation of composer and copyist is unparalleled in the autographs, though it is found in many of the conducting scores at Hamburg. Another example of Smith's cooperation is in the autograph of *Alcina* (1735), where he wrote the clefs and text of most of the recitatives.

It seems likely that besides his own autographs Handel kept

---

[1] The other copyist, unidentified by name, has been called S_1 by Professor Larsen, who has distinguished twelve others, in some degree connected with Smith, and has designated them S_2 to S_{13}. Only S_1 and S_5 worked regularly for Handel.

(or at least had easy access to) copies of them made by authorized copyists. He used to write into these copies alterations and annotations. There are many such at Hamburg, some in the Royal Music Library and some in the Fitzwilliam Museum: it cannot of course be stated as a certainty that they ever formed part of the 'Musick Books'. One particularly interesting example in the royal music is an incomplete score of the c. 1732 version of *Aci, Galatea e Polifemo*: pl. xii shows how Handel used one page and wrote part of it. There is also a score of *Il Pastor Fido* (*c.* 1712) with numerous pencil annotations in his hand. Both these probably belonged originally to the collection of 'conducting scores' now in Hamburg, but were separated from the rest before Schoelcher sold them.

Handel's autographs contain an exceptional wealth of chronological information of various kinds. Unfortunately, nearly half of those written before he settled in London are lost, and of those extant a number are fragmentary. We do not know, therefore, exactly when he began to evolve his system of precise dating, but it became something highly personal to him and most informative to posterity. His earliest dated autograph appears to be that of the Psalm 'Dixit dominus', on the last leaf of which he wrote: S. D. G. [soli deo gloria] G. F. Handel, 1707 li [   ] d'Aprile. Roma', but never added the day of the month. Thus the first completely dated work is another Psalm, 'Laudate pueri dominum', in D,—'S.D.G.G.F.H. 1707 il 8 Julij. Roma'. When Handel completed the Utrecht 'Te Deum' (1712) he meticulously added, after '14 Jan.', the phrase 'v. st.', i.e. 'vieux style' [old style].

It was in the autograph of the Ode for St. Cecilia's Day (1739) that Handel first introduced an individual touch—the use of an astrological sign to denote the day of the week.[1] These signs are found in practically all his later autographs (pls. ix, xiii, xvi). Once, in the autograph of *Faramondo* (1737), Handel went so far as to write, after completing Act II, 'Sontags abends üm [*sic*] 10 Uhr'— ['Sunday evening about 10 o'clock']. When writing his terminal

---

[1] The seven signs, and their equivalents, are as follows:

☽	♂	☿	♃	♀	♄	☉
Monday	Tuesday	Wednesday	Thursday	Friday	Saturday	Sunday

note to the autograph of *Susanna* (pl. xiii), he even added, for the first time, his age, 'aetatis 63': the last instance of this is in the autograph of *Jephtha*—'aetatis 66'.

The autographs of Handel's large vocal works, principally the operas and oratorios, provide more and more detail about their growth as he gradually developed the habit of dating each Act or Part. The earliest such composition of which the autograph bears date, month, and year is *Teseo* (fragmentary) which ends with the words 'Fine del Drama a Londres G F H ce 18 de Decembr 1712'. The autograph of *Tamerlano* provides a unique instance of a comprehensive date—'Fine dell'Opera. Cominciata li 3 di Luglio e finita li 23. Anno 1724'. We do not know exactly when Handel began to date each Act: the earliest autograph in which two Acts are dated is that of *Partenope* (1730). Thereafter this became a fairly regular habit (see the table on p. 26, 27).

In 1734, when composing *Ariodante*, Handel first used the word 'angefangen' (begun). He reached the final stage in the development of his precise chronological annotation in 1736 when he wrote, in the autograph of *Arminio* 'Fine dell'Opera G. F. Handel Octob^r 3 Anno 1736. Den 14 dieses vollends alles ausgefüllet'— ['The 14th of this [month] all completely filled out']. This phrase— and several variants such as 'völlig geendet' or 'völlig geendiget' (pl. xiii) [fully finished], 'völlig ausgefüllt', 'geendiget auszufüllen'— all denote the last of his processes of composition. Having first written the melodic line for first violin or voice and the bass, and having dated each Act, he would go back after a short interval and fill in the middle parts, and then often add a second date. During the latter process, he would add instructions to the copyist as required, put in marks of expression, and write the music for the recitatives.

Although Handel did not date with the day and the month the two stages of his work on each Act, or Part, of every work in three sections, he did so often enough to give us a lot of information about his rate of progress in composition at various times during his career. There are extant the autographs of thirty-two such works with the sections dated, as shown in the table on pages 26 and 27.

Work and year of composition	Number of pages in the autograph	Begun	Act I finished in draft	Act I fully completed	Act II finished in draft	Act II fully completed	Act III finished in draft	Act III fully completed	The whole fully completed
Tamerlano (1724)	256	3 July							23 July*
Partenope (1730)	210			14 Jan.*		30 Dec.*			6 Feb.*
Poro (1730–1)	148			23 Dec.*		10 Nov.*			16 Jan.*
Orlando (1732)	178								20 Nov.*
Ariodante (1734)	192	12 Aug.		5 Jan.*		9 Sept.*			24 Oct.*
Alexander's Feast** (1736)	176					17 Jan.*			
Atalanta (1736)	136			9 April*		14 April*			22 April*
Arminio (1736)	162		19 Sept.		26 Sept.		3 Oct.		14 Oct.
Giustino (1736)	182	14 Aug.	29 Aug.		3 Sept.		7 Sept.		15–20 Oct.
Berenice (1736–7)	154	18 Dec.	27 Dec.		7 Jan.		18 Jan.		27 Jan.
Il Trionfo del Tempo (1737)	78 (fragmentary)	2 March						14 March*	
Faramondo (1737)	172	15 Nov.		28 Nov.*		4 Dec.*		24 Dec.*	
Serse (1737–8)	234	26 Dec.	9 Jan.		25 Jan.		6 Feb.		14 Feb.
Saul (1738)	266	23 July (folio 9)			8 Aug.	28 Aug.	27 Sept.* folio 115		
Imeneo (1738–40)	126 (incomplete)			14 Sept.*	1–11 Oct.	1 Nov.	20 Sept.*		
Israel in Egypt** (1738)	146	15 Oct.	20 Oct.	28 Oct.					(later chorus, 10 Oct 1740)
L'Allegro, il Penseroso ed il Moderato (1740)									

Work	Folios					
Deidamia (1740)	172	27 Oct.	1 Nov.*	7 Nov.*	begun 14 Oct.	20 Nov.*
Messiah (1741)	280	22 Aug.	28 Aug.	6 Sept.	12 Sept.	14 Sept.
Samson (1741–2)	298		29 Sept.*	11 Oct.*	29 Oct.* (later revision 12 Oct. 1742)	
Semele (1743)	234	3 June	13 June	20 June		4 July
Joseph (1743)	244	19 July	26 Aug.	12 Sept.		
Hercules (1744)	266		30 July	11 Aug.	17 Aug.	? (the date cut away)
Belshazzar (1744)	334	23 Aug.	3 Sept.	begun 25 July / 10 Sept.*	15 Sept.	
Judas Maccabaeus (1746)	276	8 or 9 July	21 July	2 Aug.	11 Aug.	
Alexander Balus (1747)	226	1 June		24 June	30 June	4 July
Joshua (1747)	208	19 July	30 July*	8 Aug.*	18 Aug.	19 Aug.
Solomon (1748)	276	5 May (folio 6)	23 May	26 May	13 June	13 June
Susanna (1748)	268	11 July	21 July	9 Aug.	21 Aug.	24 Aug.
Theodora (1749)	226	28 June	5 July	11 July	17 July	31 July
Choice of Hercules (1750)**	126	28 June				5 July
Jephtha (1751)	268	21 Jan.	2 Feb.	27 Feb.	begun 18 June	30 Aug.

* The date which Handel often wrote at the end of an Act (or Part) refers to one of two stages in the completion of the music—the draft, or the filling in of the orchestration, etc. Where it is uncertain to which of these the date refers, it has been printed across the line.

** In two Acts only.

Although this table has many gaps in the sequence of dates, it gives nevertheless an arresting picture of Handel's prodigious fertility and speed of composition. Many biographies cite *Messiah*, written in twenty-five days, as an instance, but fail to mention others equally remarkable. *Tamerlano*, only twenty-four pages less in autograph, was completed in twenty-one days. In 1736 Handel finished *Atalanta, Arminio, Giustino*, and *Alexander's Feast*, to a total of 682 pages, between the beginning of January and the middle of October. Perhaps his greatest feat of sustained creative effort occurred in 1744 when he wrote the 600 pages comprising the autographs of *Hercules* and *Belshazzar* in barely two months. Of the latter he wrote the fifty-one pages of Act 2 in seven days.

It is certain that before Handel began the first outline of any major work, he made numerous sketches and drafts, of which only a few survive, mostly, as already mentioned, now in the Fitzwilliam Museum. One leaf of especial interest bears sketches for several numbers in *Messiah* (pl. xiv). Even allowing for this aid, Handel's productivity was all the more remarkable when it is remembered that his periods of composition were fitted into a busy life of conducting. Not all his large-scale vocal works were of equally high quality, nor did his inspiration always flow with equal smoothness. The autograph of *Saul*, for instance, with numerous fiercely made changes (pl. xv) and much re-arrangement, shows how difficult Handel sometimes found it to give final shape to a masterpiece.

There is no sequence of dated instrumental works which can be compared with the vocal, except for the Concerti Grossi, Opus 6, of which all twelve fortunately survive in autograph complete but for the ending of number five. The terminal dates show that Handel wrote the set in thirty-two days between 29 September and 30 October 1739, to a total of 144 pages (pl. xvi).

It may not be entirely fanciful to see a relationship between the character of Handel's musical calligraphy and the nature of his genius. In a masterpiece of his maturity such as *Hercules*, the notes with their bold heads and the clusters of thick-stemmed quavers and semiquavers, all slanting vigorously across the page (pl. xvii), surely reflect the powerful drive of his creative imagination. When he was working at white heat, or under pressure, Handel not infrequently found that in preparing the outline score he had misjudged the space he would require. Consequently, when he came to fill in the orchestration, he had to extend the staves into the margin (pls. xv, xvii, xviii), which also provided space for additions and corrections (pl. xv).

Something of the vividness of Handel's inspiration can be seen in the autographs of his dramatic works. As a man of the theatre, he clearly visualized the action in progress while writing the score, in which he often wrote out the stage-directions in full. One of many notable instances occurs in *Belshazzar*, at the foot of fol. 105 verso:

As he is speaking, a hand appears writing upon the wall over against him: he sees it, turns pale with fear, drops the Bowl of Wine, falls back in his seat trembling from head to foot and his knees knocking against each other (pl. xviii).

Again, in the opera *Poro*, there is a detailed, vivid description of a battle scene [translation]:

The Indians attack the Macedonians on the flank who rout them at once and Timagene vanishes among the crowd, leaving on the stage only Poro and Alessandro who fight together. Alessandro pursues Poro offstage. At the first attack of the Indians Gandarte, with a troop of Pioneers, goes onto the bridge, and destroys it at two ends which join the banks: then throwing the sword and the helmet-crest into the river, he throws himself into the river, followed by the Pioneers (pl. vi *b*).

Yet, whatever excitement Handel may have felt when writing his scores, it was always controlled and did not affect his preciseness. His meticulous dating of successive Acts in many dramatic works has already been described. In one of the important autographs, that of *Solomon*, he went so far as to indicate the timing of each Act— 50 minutes for Act 1, 40 for Act 2 (pl. xix), and 40 again for Act 3. This appears to be the only autograph in which he included detail of this kind. His detailed instructions for performance are well exemplified in the score of the 'Fireworks' Music (pl. xx).

The autographs reveal many other aspects of Handel's genius and character such as his sensitivity to the niceties of word setting, his habit of altering and interchanging the music of his dramatic works at successive revivals, his search for musical perfection and refinement as revealed by alterations and cancellations. These are large and fascinating topics which lie rather beyond the scope of this booklet. But if from what has been said in these pages there emerges one salient aspect of Handel's character, it is surely the exceptionally methodical basis of his approach to the manifold tasks of composition. Without it, he could hardly have combined his immense fertility with such high musical quality. Truly does he exemplify Carlyle's phrase—'genius, which means transcendent capacity of taking trouble, first of all'.

LIST OF BOOKS AND ARTICLES

ANON. [Often erroneously attributed to William Coxe.] *Ancedotes of George Frederick Handel and John Christopher Smith.* London, 1799.

ANON. 'The Royal Music Library at Buckingham Palace.' In *The Musical Times*, July 1902, pp. 451–5.

COOPERSMITH, Jacob M. 'The First Gesamtausgabe: Dr. Arnold's Edition of Handel's Works.' In *Notes*, June, 1947, pp. 277–88, and Sept. 1947, pp. 439–49.

DEAN, Winton. *Handel's Dramatic Oratorios and Masques.* London, 1959.

DEUTSCH, Otto E. *Handel. A documentary biography.* London, 1955.

FULLER-MAITLAND, John A., and MANN, Arthur H. *Catalogue of the Music in the Fitzwilliam Museum, Cambridge.* [The section describing the Handel Manuscripts by A. H. Mann.] London, 1893.

HALL, James A. 'John Christopher Smith, Handel's Friend and Secretary'. In *The Musical Times*, March 1955, pp. 132–4.

HIRSCH, Paul. 'Dr. Arnold's Handel Edition (1787–1797).' In *The Music Review*, May 1947, pp. 106–16.

KING, A. Hyatt. 'Frederick Nicolay, Chrysander, and the Royal Music Library.' In *The Monthly Musical Record*, Jan.–Feb. 1959, pp. 13–24.

—— *Some British Collectors of Music, c. 1600–1960.* Cambridge, 1964.

—— *William Barclay Squire, 1855–1927.* [Reprinted from the Transactions of the Bibliographical Society, *The Library*, March 1957]. London, 1957.

LARSEN, Jens P. *Handel's 'Messiah'. Origins. Composition. Sources.* London, 1957.

LONSDALE, Roger. *Dr. Charles Burney. A literary biography.* Oxford, 1965.

MANN, Arthur H. 'An Account of the Handel MSS. in the Fitzwilliam Museum at Cambridge.' In *The Musical Times*, Dec. 1893, Handel Supplement, pp. 16–19.

PARRATT, Sir Walter. 'The Handel Autographs at Buckingham Palace.' In *The Musical Times*, Dec. 1893, Handel Supplement, pp. 14–16.

ROCKSTRO, William S. *The Life of George Frederick Handel.* London, 1883.

SCHOELCHER, Victor. *The Life of Handel.* [Translated from the French by James Lowe.] London [1857].

SHAW, Harold Watkins. *A Textual and Historical Companion to Handel's 'Messiah'.* London, 1965.

SMITH, William C. Catalogue of [Handel's] Works. In *Handel. A Symposium.* Edited by Gerald Abraham. London, 1954, pp. 275–310.

—— *A Handelian's Notebook.* London, 1965.

—— 'Handeliana.' In *Music and Letters*, April 1950, pp. 125–32.

—— 'More Handeliana.' In *Music and Letters*, Jan. 1953, pp. 11–24.

SQUIRE, William Barclay. *Catalogue of the King's Music Library.* Part I. The Handel Manuscripts. London, 1927.

STREATFEILD, Richard A. *Handel Autographs at the British Museum.* London, 1912.

In the Name of god Amen.

I George Frideric Handel considering the
Uncertainty of human Life doe make this my
Will in manner following.
viz.

I give and bequeath unto my Servant
Peter le Blond, my Clothes and Linnen, and
three hundred Pounds sterl: and to my other
servants a year Wages.

I give and bequeath to Mr Christopher Smith
my large Harpsicord, my Little House Organ, my
Musick Books, and five hundred Pounds sterl:

Item I give and bequeath to Mr James Hunter

five hundred Pounds sterl:

1. The first page of the private copy of Handel's will, written in
his hand and dated 1 June 1750. He has possibly added, and then
deleted, the word 'senior' after the name Christopher Smith.
(18.0 × 22.5cm.)

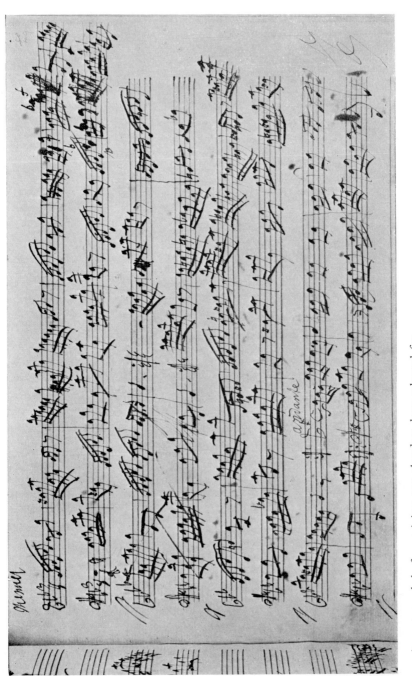

11. An autograph leaf containing two sketches, later adapted for the minuet in the overture, and 'Brighter scenes I seek above', in *Jephtha*. (Fol. 49 recto of a volume of miscellaneous instrumental works.) (30 × 23 cm.)

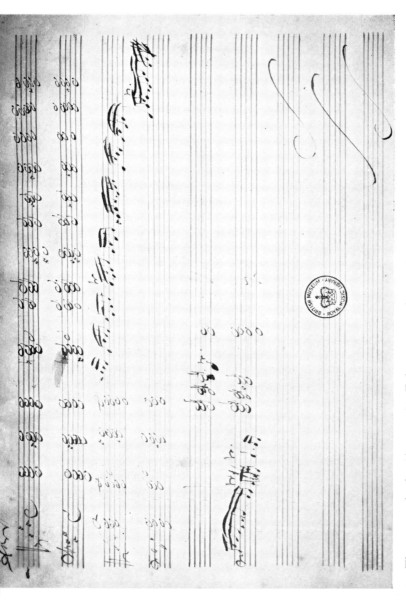

III. The autograph of an 'Arpeggio' in F sharp minor, of uncertain date, for harpsichord. (Fol. 62 verso of a volume of miscellaneous instrumental works.) (29.0 × 23.4 cm.)

IV. A list of lacunae inserted in the autograph score of *Deborah* and written c. 1780 by Frederick Nicolay. (27.0 × 42.5 cm.)

. Part of fol. 16 recto of the autograph of *Rodelinda*, 1725,
1owing the tab left by the binder when trimming round the music
ritten in the margin. (29.5 × 22.5 cm.)

(a)

(b)

VIa. Part of a leaf of memoranda in Handel's autograph, of uncertain date, including the music of a London cry 'Buy any matches'. (29.0 × 22.5 cm.)

VIb. Part of fol. 34 recto of the autograph of *Poro*, 1730–31, showing the stage direction 'Gli Indiani attacano per fianco, etc.' ('The Indians attack the Macedonians on the flank, etc.')

VII. Part of fol. 3 recto of the autograph of 'Laudate pueri dominum', c. 1702, in F major. This is probably Handel's earliest extant autograph and is written in a small hand. (21.5 × 32.5 cm.)

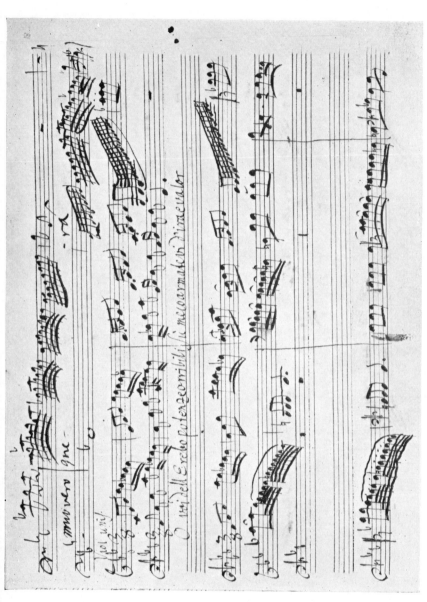

VIII. Fol. 18 recto of the autograph of *La Resurrezione*, 1708, showing the bold but controlled style of Handel's writing at this time (25.6 × 11.2 cm.)

Fol. 91 verso of the autograph of *Jephtha*, 1751. Handel's
te states that he ceased writing at the end of this page, on 13
bruary, because of worsening eyesight. He failed to add stems to
ne of the note-heads. (29.1 × 24.0 cm.)

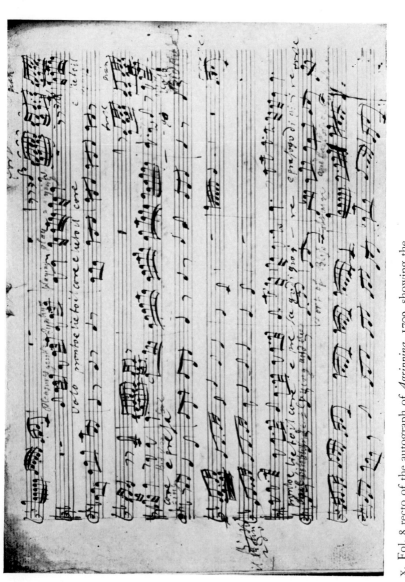

x. Fol. 8 recto of the autograph of *Agrippina*, 1709, showing the song 'Volo pronto' above the words of which Handel added an English text 'Pleasure's gentle zephyrs playing', possibly in 1757 when the song was introduced into his oratorio *The Triumph of Time and Truth*. (29.6 × 22.0 cm.)

XI. Part of fol. 16 recto of the autograph of *Deborah*, 1733. On the upper six staves the music is written by J. C. Smith the elder, the words by Handel. On the two lowest staves the music is written by Handel, the words by Smith. (27·4 × 42·7 cm.)

XII. Fol. 67 recto of a copyists' score of Handel's serenata *Aci, Galatea e Polifemo*, c. 1732. On the upper six staves the music and the pencilled correction of the name above the staves are written by Handel and the words by Smith. On the four lowest staves

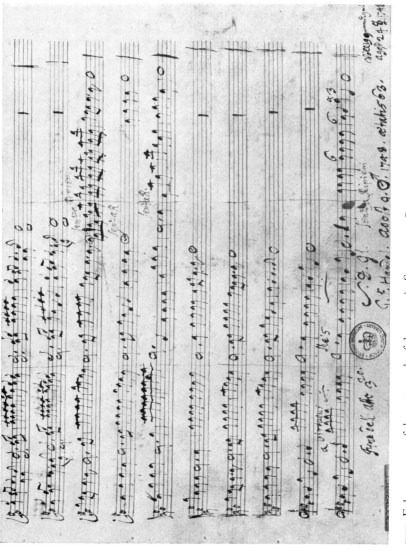

XIII. Fol. 134 verso of the autograph of the oratorio *Susanna*, 1748,
showing Handel's final inscription, including his age 'aetatis 63'.
(29.7 × 23.8 cm.)

xɪv. An autograph leaf containing sketches for 'He was despised', and 'Let all the angels', in *Messiah*, 1741. The eighth stave bears the music of a tune 'Der arme Irische Junge'. The note at the foot is in the hand of Vincent Novello. (27.5 × 22.7 cm.)

xv. Fol. 52 recto of the autograph of *Saul*, 1738, showing Handel's
heavy corrections. (23.5 × 29.9 cm.)

XVI. The last page of the autograph of the Concerto Grosso in C minor, Op. 6, No. 8, 1739. (Fol. 112 recto of a volume of concertos.) (29.0 × 23.8 cm.)

II. Fol. 105 recto of the autograph of the oratorio *Hercules*, 1744.
Handel's writing slopes strongly across the page. (29.5 × 23.8 cm.)

XVIII. Part of fol. 105 verso of the autograph of *Belshazzar*, 1744, showing the stage direction 'As he is speaking, a Hand appears, etc.' (29.6 × 24.0 cm.)

. Fol. 87 verso of the autograph of *Solomon*, 1748, showing the
 of Part II, with Handel's note of the approximate timing—
minutes'. (30.5 × 24.2 cm.)

xx. A page of the autograph for the 'Music for the Royal Fireworks',
1749. (Fol. 27 recto of a volume of miscellaneous instrumental
works.) At the foot Handel has written detailed instructions for
performance. (23.5 × 30.0 cm.)